TURKMENISTAN

TURKMENISTAN

Prepared by
Geography Department

Lerner Publications Company
Minneapolis

Series editors: Mary M. Rodgers, Tom Streissguth,
  Colleen Sexton
Photo researcher: Kathy Raskob
Designer: Zachary Marell

Our thanks to the following for their help in preparing
and checking the text of this book: Dr. Craig ZumBrunnen,
Department of Geography, University of Washington;
Dr. Nicholas Hayes, Director of International Studies,
Hamline University; Dr. Larry Clark, Department of Uralic
and Altaic Studies, Indiana University.

Terms in **bold** appear in a glossary that starts on page 52.

Pronunciation Guide

Bolsoj Balchan	bohl-SHOW-ee bahl-CHAN
Chardzhou	char-JOO
Dzhunaid	joo-NAY-id
Genghis	GEN-giss
glasnost	GLAHZ-nost
Geok-Tepe	geohk—teh-PAY
Kara-Bogaz Gol	KAH-rah—boh-GAHZ GOHL
Khodzhamuradov	koh-jah-MUR-ah-dov
Krasnovodsk	kras-noh-VOHTSK
Makhtumkuli	mahkh-TOOM-koo-lee
perestroika	pehr-eh-STROY-kah
Tekke	tehk-KEH
Zoroastrianism	zor-uh-WAHS-tree-uhn-izm

LIBRARY OF CONGRESS CATALOGING-IN-PUBLICATION DATA

    Turkmenistan/prepared by Geography Department, Lerner Publi-
cations Company.
        p.   cm.—(Then & now)
    Includes index.
    Summary: Discusses the history, geography, politics, ethnic
mixture, economics, and possible future of this former Soviet
Socialist Republic, now an independent nation.
    ISBN 0-8225-2813-4 (lib. bdg.)
    1. Turkmenistan—Juvenile literature. [1. Turkmenistan.]
I. Lerner Publications Company. Geography Dept. II. Series:
Then & now (Minneapolis, Minn.)
DK933.T82 1993
958'.5—dc20   92-40236
                                                                  CIP
                                                                  AC

Manufactured in the United States of America
1 2 3 4 5 6 98 97 96 95 94 93

• CONTENTS •

A camel grazes along the banks of the Kara Kum Canal, a long artificial waterway that irrigates farmland in Turkmenistan.

''[Turkmenistan should be] neither Islamic nor Soviet but a secular, democratic state.''

Adbu Kuliyev,
Foreign Minister of Turkmenistan

In 1992, the Soviet Union would have celebrated the 75th anniversary of the revolution of 1917. During that revolt, political activists called **Communists** overthrew the czar (ruler) and the government of the **Russian Empire**. The revolution of 1917 was the first step in establishing the 15-member **Union of Soviet Socialist Republics (USSR)**.

The Soviet Union stretched from eastern Europe across northern Asia and contained nearly 300 million people. Within this vast nation, the Communist government guaranteed housing, education, health care, and lifetime employment. Communist leaders told farmers and factory workers that Soviet citizens owned all property in common. The new nation quickly **industrialized**, meaning it built many new factories and upgraded existing ones. It also modernized and enlarged its farms. In addition, the USSR created a huge, well-equipped military force that allowed it to become one of the most powerful nations in the world.

Wearing traditional clothing, Turkmen merchants offer brightly colored fabrics for sale in Ashgabat (once spelled Ashkhabad), the capital of Turkmenistan.

(Left) *Cranes mark the place in Ashgabat where a new mosque (Islamic house of prayer) is under construction. Since gaining independence from Soviet rule in 1991, Turkmen are reviving age-old customs and openly practicing the Islamic religion.* (Below) *Some Turkmen families live in the Kara Kum Desert, which dominates the center of the country.*

The **Turkmen Soviet Socialist Republic** was brought into the Soviet Union in 1924. Also known as Turkmenistan, this remote desert state was one of the poorest of the Soviet republics, although it boasted fertile river valleys and plentiful energy resources. The republic's Communist government, made up of **ethnic Russians** as well as **ethnic Turkmen**, was loyal to the USSR. Nevertheless, the people of Turkmenistan remained fiercely independent. They maintained a separate identity, even when Soviet leaders forced the Turkmen to join state-owned **collective farms** and restricted the practice of Islam, their traditional religion.

By the early 1990s, the Soviet Union was in a period of rapid change and turmoil. The central government had mismanaged the economy, which was failing to provide goods. To control the various ethnic groups within the USSR, the Communists had long restricted many freedoms. People throughout the vast nation were dissatisfied, and some republics were demanding freedom from Soviet control.

As part of her on-the-job train-ing, this young Turkmen paints a wooden window frame.

These demands worried the Soviet Union's powerful, conservative Communist officials. In August 1991, several of them tried to use the Soviet military to overthrow Mikhail Gorbachev, the USSR's president. After only a few days, the attempted overthrow failed. Turkmenistan's leaders decided to support Gorbachev, who was trying to hold the nation together with a program of economic and social reforms. Despite his efforts, the USSR gradually broke apart.

In the fall of 1991, Turkmenistan's leaders proclaimed their republic's independence from Soviet rule. In December, Turkmenistan joined the **Commonwealth of Independent States**, a loose confederation of former Soviet republics. In March 1992, Turkmenistan also became a member of the **United Nations**.

Turkmenistan is following a new and independent course in political and economic affairs. Turkmen leaders have written a new constitution and have set up an elected legislature. The country is forming closer commercial ties with neighboring nations, many of which are also former Soviet republics. In addition, foreign businesses from Europe and the Middle East are interested in developing Turkmenistan's natural resources.

These new opportunities may raise Turkmenistan's standard of living. Yet the country still faces serious economic and social problems. Many skilled workers are emigrating, and Turkmenistan has poor health standards and high unemployment. In addition, many of Turkmenistan's people are demanding a greater role for Islam in their laws and society. Freedom from Soviet rule has allowed Turkmen leaders to remake their government, but independence has also caused conflict over the best way to prepare the country's citizens for the challenges of the future.

CHAPTER ONE

The Land and People of Turkmenistan

T he Republic of Turkmenistan, an independent nation in central Asia, lies in one of the world's hottest and most sparsely populated regions. An ancient Turkmen legend says that God's first gift to the world was the gift of the sun to the Turkmen. But the Turkmen were the last to receive water, and God left their land parched and dry.

A harsh climate and a vast desert have prevented settlement in much of Turkmenistan. Most of the country's people still live in oases (fertile areas fed by underground springs) and along waterways that carry precious water to small villages and farms. Turkmenistan's larger towns and cities grew along historic trading routes that linked Asia and the Middle East.

On a playing field in the capital, Turkmen and Russian boys compete in a game of soccer.

On the western border of Turkmenistan are the shores of the Caspian Sea. A large inlet on this sea is known as the Kara-Bogaz Gol (gulf). The former Soviet republics of Kazakhstan and Uzbekistan are Turkmenistan's northern neighbors. Afghanistan lies to the southeast, and Iran is to the south. Turkmenistan covers 188,455 square miles (488,098 square kilometers), an area nearly twice as large as the state of Texas or three times the size of Italy.

Large herds of goats roam the Kara Kum Desert in search of sparse pasture.

At Krasnovodsk, a port city on the shores of the Caspian Sea, a woman monitors the processing of the day's haul of fish.

The people who live in the region of Krasnovodsk call these barren clay hills the Moon Mountains, because they resemble the landscape of the moon.

• Topography and Rivers •

The Kara Kum Desert—whose name means "black sands" in Turkmen, the language of the Turkmen—is the most important feature of Turkmenistan's landscape. The world's fourth largest desert, the Kara Kum spans central Turkmenistan and stretches northward into Uzbekistan. The desert's dunes and gravelly basins lie within a wide, flat plain known as the Turanian Lowlands. Many of the dunes reach 300 feet (91 meters) in height. The people of the desert can grow crops only in oases and in areas that are irrigated by artificial canals.

West of the Kara Kum, the land gradually rises near the Caspian Sea and the Kara-Bogaz Gol. Between the desert and the sea is the small Krasnovodsk Plateau, and to the south rise the Bolsoj Balchan Mountains. South of the Kara Kum is the Kopet-Dag range, which reaches 9,652 feet (2,942 m) along the Iranian border.

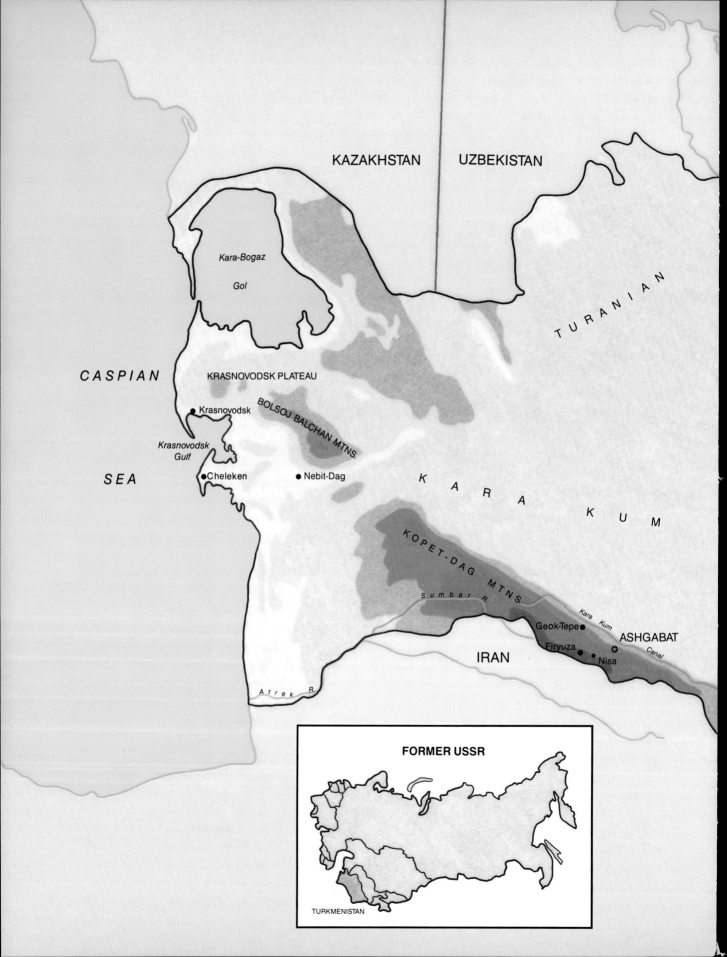

KAZAKHSTAN   UZBEKISTAN

Kara-Bogaz

Gol

CASPIAN

TURANIAN

KRASNOVODSK PLATEAU

● Krasnovodsk

BOLSOJ BALCHAN MTNS.

*Krasnovodsk
Gulf*

SEA

●Cheleken   ● Nebit-Dag

K   A   R   A

K   U   M

KOPET-DAG MTNS.

S u m b a r   R.

Kara Kum

Geok-Tepe●   ASHGABAT ✪

Firyuza● ● Nisa   Canal

IRAN

A t r e k   R.

FORMER USSR

TURKMENISTAN

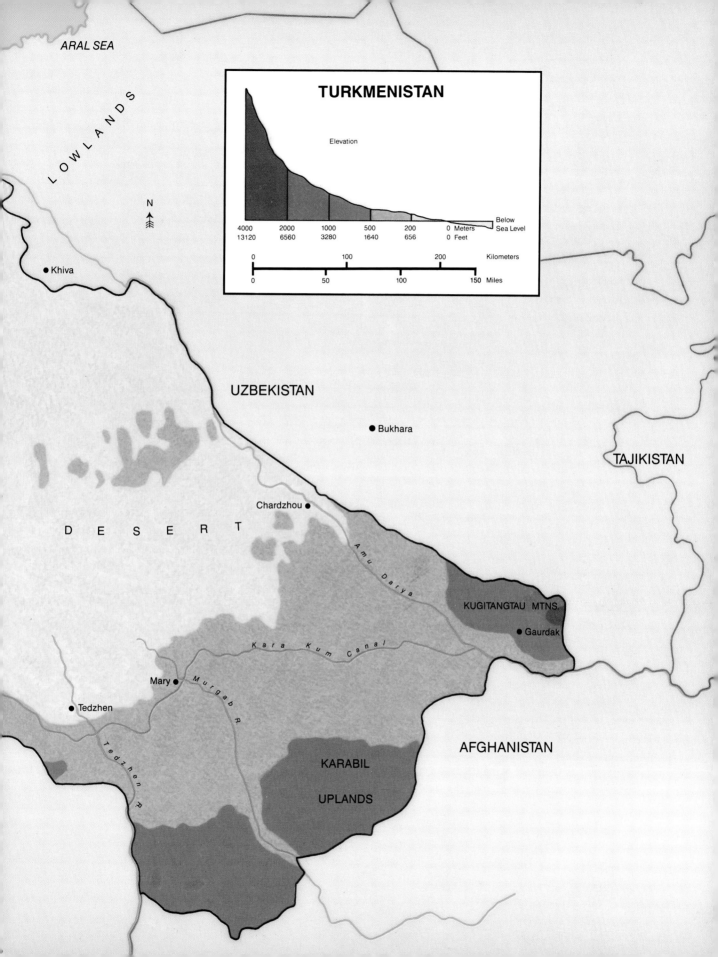

ARAL SEA

L O W L A N D S

● Khiva

N

TURKMENISTAN

Elevation

| 4000 | 2000 | 1000 | 500 | 200 | 0 | Meters | Below |
| 13120 | 6560 | 3280 | 1640 | 656 | 0 | Feet | Sea Level |

| 0 | | 100 | | 200 | | Kilometers |

| 0 | 50 | | 100 | | 150 | Miles |

UZBEKISTAN

● Bukhara

TAJIKISTAN

Chardzhou ●

D E S E R T

Amu Darya

KUGITANGTAU MTNS.

● Gaurdak

Kara Kum Canal

Mary ●

Murgab R.

● Tedzhen

Tedzhen R.

AFGHANISTAN

KARABIL

UPLANDS

In the southeast, the Kara Kum ends at an elevated plateau, where river valleys and canals sustain large towns and farms. Near the border with Afghanistan are the Karabil Uplands. To the northeast lie the foothills of the Kugitangtau Mountains, which reach 10,292 feet (3,137 m)—the highest point in Turkmenistan.

Only a few rivers flow through Turkmenistan's parched land. The country's longest waterway is the Amu Darya (River), which follows the northeastern boundary of Turkmenistan for 620 miles (997 km) before crossing into Uzbekistan and emptying into the Aral Sea. The Murgab and Tedzhen rivers enter Turkmenistan from the south and evaporate in the sands of the Kara Kum. The Atrek and Sumbar rivers have short courses in the southwest.

The Kara Kum Canal, an artificial waterway, runs nearly 700 miles (1,126 km) from the Amu Darya to Ashgabat (formerly Ashkhabad), Turkmenistan's capital, and beyond to the northwest. The canal supplies water to population centers and to farms that grow cotton, a crop requiring extensive irrigation. Begun during the 1950s, the Kara Kum Canal is now the world's longest irrigation canal. Engineers have made plans to extend this vital waterway to the Caspian Sea.

(Above) *During Turkmenistan's brief winter, snow sometimes falls in the desert and in the mountains.* (Below) *The Kara Kum Canal, which cuts a blue line across the desert, enables farmers in the area to grow orchard crops and cotton.*

(Below) **Children play in an irrigation canal that flows through the capital.** (Right) **Near the city of Chardzhou in eastern Turkmenistan, an engineer operates equipment that looks for deposits of natural gas.**

• Climate and Natural Resources •

Temperatures in Turkmenistan's dry climate are extreme. Long summer days in July average at least 90° F (32° C), while the brief winter can bring low temperatures of −20° F (−29° C) in January and February. In Ashgabat, summer temperatures often reach 120° F (49° C) in the shade.

Rainfall in most of Turkmenistan averages only 3 to 4 inches (8 to 10 centimeters) per year. In the higher elevations of the south, rainfall increases to as much as 12 inches (30 cm). During winter, snow occasionally falls in the desert and in the mountains of southern Turkmenistan.

Although it lacks water, Turkmenistan abounds in other natural resources. The Kara Kum Desert has deposits of oil, natural gas, sulfur, potassium, coal, lead, salt, and other minerals. Oil reserves lie along the Caspian Sea near the town of Nebit-Dag. Natural gas exists in the valley of the Amu Darya and near the city of Mary in southern Turkmenistan. Once controlled by the Soviet government, Turkmenistan's oil and gas deposits have become the new nation's most valuable source of export earnings.

When the weather is fine, this park in the capital attracts strolling Turkmen.

• Cities •

Before the 20th century, the vast majority of Turkmen were rural. Many owned herds of livestock and moved frequently from place to place in search of pasture and water. After bringing the region under its control in the 1920s, the Soviet government built new factories in Turkmenistan's scattered population centers. The growing cities also became a home for immigrants from the Soviet republics of Russia and Ukraine. About 45 percent of Turkmenistan's population of 3.9 million now live in urban areas.

(Above) **On October 5, 1948, an unusually strong earthquake leveled almost all of the mud and brick houses of Ashgabat. This monument honors the thousands of people killed during the disaster.** (Below) **Boats crowd the docks in Krasnovodsk.**

Ashgabat (population 398,000) lies in an oasis at the foot of the Kopet-Dag Mountains. In 1881, the army of the Russian Empire built a fortress on the site, which had been occupied by a village. Russian merchants and traders arrived after engineers constructed a railroad to connect the growing city to other towns in central Asia. The railway also brought settlers from Persia (modern Iran) and from Armenia, a region west of the Caspian Sea.

After a devastating earthquake in 1948, the people of Ashgabat rebuilt their city. Parks and botanical gardens now provide residents with pleasant open spaces. Ashgabat also boasts theaters, museums, and a university. Eighteen miles (29 km) to the west lie the ruins of Nisa, an ancient city that attracts tourists and archaeologists. Food processing and silk weaving are important industries in Ashgabat. The capital's factories also make carpets, glass, and machinery.

Chardzhou (population 161,000) is an industrial and agricultural hub in the Amu Darya Valley. During the 20th century, the city grew rapidly as a center of trade in cotton, a crop raised on farms along the Amu Darya. Chardzhou's textile plants still process cotton for the region. The city also has chemical factories, as well as shipyards for the construction of river barges.

Southwest of Chardzhou, along an important railway line in the Murgab Valley, lies the town of Mary (population 74,000). In ancient times, this was the site of Merv, the capital of the region of Margiana. Merv later became an important stop along the **Silk Road**, a trade route between Asia and Europe. After Russian settlers arrived in the late 19th century, Mary became a hub of cotton growing in the Murgab Valley.

Turkmenistan's largest port is Krasnovodsk, a city of 55,000 on the small Krasnovodsk Gulf on the

Caspian Sea. The port grew around a fort built by the Russians in 1717. Tankers carrying Turkmenistan's oil and natural gas dock at Krasnovodsk, which also exports cotton and fish.

• Ethnic Heritage •

The ethnic Turkmen of modern times descend from the **Oguz**. These ancient Turkic peoples migrated from eastern Asia into central Asia and the Middle East in the 7th and 8th centuries A.D. The Turkmen have close ties of language and culture to other descendants of the Oguz who now live in Iran, Afghanistan, and Azerbaijan, a former Soviet republic west of the Caspian Sea. Turkmen account for 72 percent of Turkmenistan's population, and nearly 200,000 Turkmen live outside their homeland.

(Left) *As one of her daily chores, a rural woman milks the family camel. Valued for their milk and meat, these animals are ideal desert dwellers that can live for days on very little water and food.* (Above) *Carrying a large bundle on her head, a young girl makes her way down a village street.*

(Above) *Horse racing is a popular sport among Turkmen. Here, jockeys gallop to the finish line at an arena in Ashgabat. They ride Argamak horses, a breed prized for its grace and stamina.* (Below) *Russian and Turkmen boys share a loaf of bread on their way home from school.*

The Turkmen divide themselves into several clans that have frequently fought among themselves during the region's history. The largest clan—the **Tekke**—now numbers about 500,000. Members of the Tekke dominated Turkmenistan's Communist leadership and still make up a large class of government officials.

Turkmenistan is also home to Uzbeks, Kazakhs, Armenians, and Tatars. About 10 percent of Turkmenistan's people are Slavs, including ethnic Russians and **ethnic Ukrainians**. Most of Turkmenistan's Slavs—who began settling in central Asia in the 19th century—live in cities and towns. Russians form 40 percent of the population of Ashgabat. Nevertheless, many Slavs have left Turkmenistan, fearing new laws that would favor Turkmen-speakers for jobs, political positions, and educational opportunities.

Newlyweds follow local tradition by posing with their families in front of a statue of the 18th-century Turkmen poet and philosopher Makhtumkuli.

At an international folk festival, a Turkmen plays her dutar, a pear-shaped, guitarlike instrument with 13 to 20 frets and 2 strings.

• Religion and Festivals •

Islam, a religion founded by the Arab prophet Muhammad, unites the people of central Asia in a common bond of faith and social customs. In the 8th century, an Arab invasion from the Middle East brought Islam to the region. The Turkmen, who had converted to Islam by the 10th century, belong to the Sunni branch, as do Kazakhs, Uzbeks, and other central Asian Muslims (followers of Islam). Members of the Sunni sect accept Islamic leaders who are not related to Muhammad. Shiite Muslims, who are a majority in Azerbaijan and Iran, follow only leaders descended from Muhammad's family.

Islam rests on the five duties of declaring faith, praying five times daily, giving to the poor, fasting, and making a pilgrimage to Mecca, a city in the Middle Eastern kingdom of Saudi Arabia. Mosques—Islamic houses of prayer and meditation—have been built throughout Turkmenistan. The Turkmen people also celebrate births, weddings, and other important events with traditional ceremonies.

Under Soviet rule, Islam came under sharp restrictions. The Communist government closed many mosques and banned public religious ceremonies. Many Muslims in Turkmenistan are now pressing for changes in their laws and government that would reflect Islamic beliefs and customs. In addition, Islamic political parties are represented in the country's government.

Russian and Ukrainian settlers brought the Eastern Orthodox branch of Christianity to Turkmenistan. The Soviet Union also restricted this religion, but the Orthodox faith survived. Orthodox churches remain open in Turkmenistan's cities and large towns.

(Above) *Soviet leaders encouraged loyalty to Communist ideals through posters in the workplace.* (Right) *Throughout Turkmenistan, new and reopened mosques are reintroducing the people to the teachings and prayers of the Islamic faith.*

• Language, Education, and Health •

Turkmeni is one of several Turkic tongues spoken in central Asia. Languages related to Turkmeni include Uzbek, Kazakh, and Kyrgyz. The Arabs brought their own system of writing to central Asia when they invaded the region in the 8th century. Although the Arabs later retreated, the Turkic peoples eventually adopted Arabic lettering, which was used in the Koran (the Islamic holy book).

After the central Asian republics joined the Soviet Union in the 1920s, the Soviet government introduced Cyrillic, the alphabet used to write Russian and other Slavic languages. The Soviets prohibited the use of Arabic lettering to discourage communication among the central Asian republics. In addition, Russian became the main language of education in the area's public schools.

(Above) *Vocational schools in Turkmenistan offer training courses in bricklaying.* (Below) *In Ashgabat, a student strolls in front of Turkmenistan's modern music school.*

At Firyuza, a city along the Iranian border in southern Turkmenistan, a pupil shows her classmates Turkmen words written with the Cyrillic alphabet. The nation is gradually replacing Cyrillic with the Latin alphabet.

Few Turkmen learned to speak Russian, and as a result few gained positions of authority under Soviet rule. After Turkmenistan won independence, schools and the government adopted the Turkmeni language. Many ethnic Russians fear that the new government will require managers and officials to be fluent in Turkmen. The government of Turkmenistan has already begun the long process of replacing the Cyrillic alphabet with Latin lettering, which is used for writing Turkish.

In the early 20th century, most ethnic Turkmen could not read or write. Some young students attended madrasas—Islamic schools where pupils learned to recite the Koran, as well as works of literature and poetry. Few rural or nomadic families sent their children to madrasas, however, and Turkmenistan had no public school system.

The Soviet government built new public schools in Turkmenistan's cities and required all children to attend school. Several institutions of higher education were founded in Ashgabat, including Gorky University. By the early 1990s, the government had also built medical and agricultural schools, as well as the 12 institutes that make up the Academy of Sciences. The Soviet emphasis on public education has raised the literacy rate in Turkmenistan to 98 percent.

The Soviets also introduced a health-care system to improve the region's poor living conditions. The rate of infant mortality—93 deaths per 1,000 births—is still the highest among the former Soviet republics. Medical clinics have been built in the nation's largest cities, but rural areas and villages still lack medicines and doctors. Life expectancy in Turkmenistan is 65 years, a low figure for central Asia. Nevertheless, the country's population is growing rapidly. At the current growth rate of 2.7 percent, it will double in just 26 years.

Young women receive on-the-job training as house painters.

CHAPTER TWO

Turkmenistan's Story

Humans have lived in Turkmenistan since prehistoric times. Archaeologists have found Stone-Age tools along the Caspian Sea shore and near the modern port of Krasnovodsk. The remains of farming settlements in the Kopet-Dag Mountains date back 8,000 years. The ancient cultivators in this region used the mountain streams to irrigate their crops. They also survived by herding livestock and by hunting wild game.

As early societies learned to make pottery and metal tools, they began to trade with other peoples of central Asia. But this profitable trade also attracted foreign invaders. By the 6th century B.C., the powerful Persian Empire had established the provinces of Parthia and Margiana, regions in what is now Turkmenistan. From their base south of the Kopet-Dag range, the Persians controlled trade through central Asia and subdued the many nomadic peoples who lived on Turkmenistan's arid plains.

Visitors walk along a winding stone road to reach the ruins of Nisa, the capital of the Parthian kingdom. The nomadic Scythians established Parthia in the 3rd century B.C.. The realm eventually covered the territory of present-day Turkmenistan and Iran.

• Early Rulers •

In the 4th century B.C., the Persian Empire was defeated by the army of Alexander the Great, a brilliant military commander from Macedonia in southern Europe. In 330 B.C., Alexander marched northward into central Asia and founded the city of Alexandria near the Murgab River. Located on an important trade route, Alexandria later became the city of Merv (modern Mary). The ruins of Alexander's ancient city are still visible along the banks of the Murgab.

Nisa lies west of Ashgabat. Excavations at the site have uncovered fortress walls, marble statues, ivory drinking cups, and agricultural records.

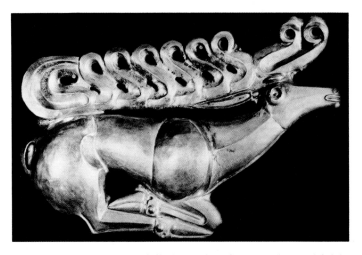

Scythian artisans were skilled metalworkers, producing lifelike decorative items, such as this gold medallion in the shape of a mythical animal.

After Alexander's death in 323 B.C., his generals fought for control of his empire, which quickly fell apart. The Scythians—fierce, nomadic warriors from the north—then established the kingdom of Parthia, which covered present-day Turkmenistan and Iran. The Parthian kings ruled their domain from the ancient city of Nisa. At its height, Parthia extended south and west as far as the Indus River in modern India.

These walls are part of the ruins of Merv (present-day Mary). The city was once an important stop on the ancient Silk Road, a trade route that transported goods between China and Europe. The complex of buildings included palaces, temples, tombs, and schools, all of which indicate that Merv was a cultural, political, and commercial center.

Parthia fell in A.D. 224 to the Sasanian rulers of Persia. At the same time, several groups—including the Alans and the Huns—were moving into Turkmenistan from the east and north. A branch of the Huns wrested control of southern Turkmenistan from the Sasanian Empire in the 5th century A.D.

• The Arrival of the Oguz •

Although Turkmenistan was still populated mostly by nomadic herders, permanent settlements were prospering in the fertile river valleys. Farmers raised grains, vegetables, and fruits along the Amu Darya, and Merv and Nisa became centers of sericulture (the raising of silkworms). A busy caravan route, connecting China and the city of Baghdad (in modern Iraq), passed through Merv. In addition,

Linking China and Europe, the 4,000-mile (6,400-km) Silk Road thrived from the 2nd century B.C. to the 8th century A.D. Caravans brought fine silk fabric westward, while horses, glass, wool, gold, and silver made the journey eastward. Few merchants traveled the entire route. Instead, using camels, oxen, donkeys, and horses, caravan drivers moved goods from city to city with the help of local brokers, such as those who worked in Merv.

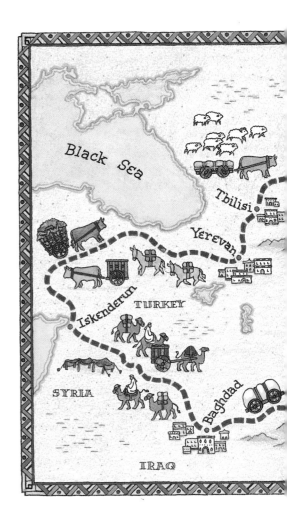

merchants, traders, and missionaries introduced the religions of Buddhism and Zoroastrianism to the region.

Central Asia came under Arab control after a series of invasions in the late 7th and early 8th centuries. Meanwhile, the Oguz—the ancestors of the Turkmen—were migrating from eastern Asia into central Asia, the Middle East, and Asia Minor (modern Turkey). The Arab conquest brought the Islamic religion to the Oguz and to the other peoples of central Asia.

By the 11th century, the Oguz were pushing to the south and west, and the Arabs were retreating from Turkmenistan. In 1040, the Seljuk clan of the Oguz established the Seljuk Empire, with its capital at Merv. At one time, the Seljuk realm stretched all the way to Baghdad. Other Oguz groups moved west across the Caspian Sea, settling in Azerbaijan and in Asia Minor, where they joined the Seljuk Turks in establishing the Ottoman Empire. After mixing with the settled peoples in Turkmenistan, the Oguz living north of the Kopet-Dag Mountains gradually became known as the Turkmen.

In the 11th and 12th centuries, the main centers of Turkmen culture were at Khiva in the north (now in Uzbekistan) and at Merv in the south. Khiva controlled the cities and farming estates of the lower Amu Darya Valley. Merv became a crossroads of trade in silks and spices between Asia and the

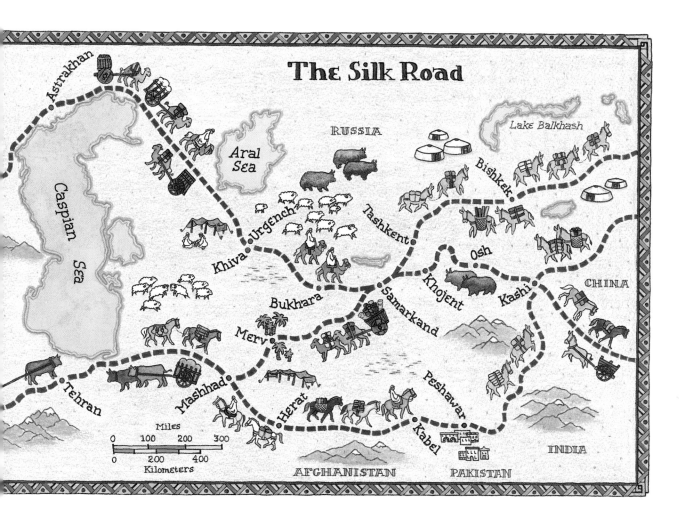

Middle East. This business created vast wealth in the ancient city, where the Seljuk rulers built fabulous mosques and palaces. At the same time, a growing class of wealthy traders and landowners was challenging the Seljuks for control of Turkmenistan.

• Mongol Invasions •

In 1157, during a revolt of powerful landowners, the Seljuk Empire collapsed. The leaders of Khiva took control of Turkmenistan, but their reign was brief. In 1221, central Asia suffered a disastrous invasion by Mongol warriors who were sweeping across the region from their base in eastern Asia.

Under their commander Genghis Khan, the Mongols conquered Khiva and burned the city of Merv to the ground. The Mongol leader ordered the massacre of Merv's inhabitants as well as the destruction of Turkmenistan's farms and irrigation works. The Turkmen who survived the invasion retreated northward to the plains of Kazakhstan or eastward to the shores of the Caspian Sea.

After Genghis Khan's death in 1227, the Mongols lost control of Turkmenistan. Small, semi-independent states arose under the rule of the region's landowners. In the 1370s, the Mongol leader Timur (known as Tamerlane in Europe), a descendant of Genghis Khan, reconquered these states and established the Timurid Empire. But after Timur's death in 1405, this realm weakened and disappeared.

The Mongol invasions had divided the Turkmen into small clans and had pushed them into the desert. Later, as the Mongols retreated from Turkmenistan, the Turkmen fell under the control of Muslim **khans** (rulers) who established **khanates** in Bukhara (in modern Uzbekistan) and Khiva.

The rivalry between the khans and the rulers of Persia touched off centuries of war in Turkmenistan. Persians, Turkmen, and the khans fought for the scattered oases in southern Turkmenistan. From the 14th to the 17th centuries, Turkmenistan was in decline. To escape the conflicts, most Turkmen moved to the remote deserts along the borders of Persia and Afghanistan.

Mongol warriors under the command of Genghis Khan swept through central Asia in the 13th century, leveling Merv and other Turkmen cities in the process. The Mongols killed or enslaved Merv's inhabitants and destroyed the city's irrigation works. As a result, agriculture and trade declined in the region. Throughout the 13th and 14th centuries, there were frequent revolts against Mongol rule.

• Russia and Turkmenistan •

In the 18th century, after centuries of poverty and isolation, the Turkmen began to rebuild their

Writing under the name Fragi, Makhtumkuli was the first Turkmen poet to use popular Turkmeni speech in his verse. The son of a poet, he studied in the city of Khiva (now in Uzbekistan) and traveled throughout central Asia. Makhtumkuli's varied works include patriotic poems, love songs, and philosophical verse. He urged his fellow Turkmen to end their bitter infighting and to join together to make a Turkmen nation.

way of life. The poet Makhtumkuli created a literary language for the Turkmen and laid the foundations for their modern culture and traditions. Keimir-Ker, a Turkmen from the Tekke clan, led a rebellion of the Turkmen against the Persians, who were occupying most of Turkmenistan. Popular ballads and folk legends still recount the deeds of Keimir-Ker.

At this time, the Russian Empire was expanding into central Asia from the plains and forests of eastern Europe. The Russian czar (ruler) Peter the Great sent the first Russian expeditions into Turkmenistan. Peter was seeking a route for Russian trade with southern Asia and the Middle East. In 1716, however, members of a Turkmen clan murdered the czar's representatives near Khiva. Russia waited for more than a century before sending another mission into Turkmenistan.

Nevertheless, trade between Turkmen merchants and Russia continued and was helped by the building of a port on the Caspian Sea at Krasnovodsk. In 1802, members of several Turkmen clans officially became Russian subjects. During the 19th century, the Turkmen also asked for Russia's help during their frequent rebellions against the khans and against the shahs (rulers) of Persia. The Russians were seeking new markets for their goods, fertile land for the growing of cotton, and access to Turkmenistan's natural resources. As a first step in the conquest of the region, the Russians agreed to provide arms and food to the Turkmen rebels.

Russia began sending military expeditions into Turkmenistan in the second half of the 19th century. From 1863 through 1868, Russian armies defeated and **annexed** (took over) the khanates of Bukhara and Khiva. The people of western Turkmenistan—who were seeking independence from the khans—willingly joined the Russian Empire.

But the Turkmen of eastern and southern Turkmenistan fiercely resisted Russian annexation. In 1879, at Geok-Tepe near Ashkhabad (modern Ashgabat), Turkmen warriors of the Tekke clan stopped a large Russian force. Two years later, the Russians besieged Geok-Tepe, eventually capturing it as well as Ashkhabad.

By 1885, all of the Turkmen clans had submitted to Russian control. The Russians annexed Mary and pushed across Turkmenistan to the borders of Persia and Afghanistan. The building of the Transcaspian Railroad—which connected Krasnovodsk, Mary, and trading centers to the east—opened up the region for economic development.

From 1890 to 1917, Turkmenistan was part of **Russian Turkestan**, a province that included central Asia and its Muslim nationalities—the Kazakhs, the Uzbeks, the Kyrgyz, the Tajiks, and the Turkmen. Within Turkestan, however, the Turkmen had a lesser status. Their lands were defined as the **Transcaspian Region** and were ruled as a military colony. This neglect by Russia's government allowed the Turkmen to maintain their culture, language, and nomadic way of life with little interference.

In the 19th century, the Russian Empire took over Turkmenistan. But the region remained a distant province where Russians exercised little direct control. As a result, many Turkmen were able to continue following their traditional nomadic ways, living in cloth tents and herding livestock in the vast deserts.

• *War and Revolution* •

In the early 20th century, discontent with strict czarist rule spread among the people of the Russian Empire. At the same time, the empire was being drawn into a bloody international conflict. During World War I (1914–1918), the Turkmen and other peoples of central Asia moved to reclaim their homelands. A violent uprising broke out in 1916, when the Turkmen, led by Dzhunaid Khan, defeated the Russians in Khiva. The Turkmen established a national government that lasted until 1918.

A statue of the Russian Communist leader Vladimir Lenin stands in Firyuza. In the early 1900s, Lenin spearheaded the revolution that brought down the Russian Empire and that established the Union of Soviet Socialist Republics, which included the Turkmen Soviet Socialist Republic (SSR).

In October 1917, the Communist leader Vladimir Lenin overthrew the Russian government. The Communists succeeded in taking control of Ashkhabad in the summer of 1918. In response, Dzhunaid Khan and forces loyal to the old Russian regime joined together to drive out the Communists. In July 1919, these anti-Communist allies established the independent state of **Transcaspia**.

• *Soviet Victory and Stalin's Rule* •

By the fall of 1920, however, the Communist Red Army was advancing from Tashkent (in modern Uzbekistan) and from Bukhara. The Communists gradually subdued Turkmenistan by military occupation and by putting Communist politicians in control of local governments. In 1922, the Communists founded the Union of Soviet Socialist Republics (USSR). Two years later, they established the Turkmen Soviet Socialist Republic (SSR) as a full member of the USSR.

In the late 1920s and early 1930s, the Soviet leader Joseph Stalin made harsh and sweeping changes throughout the USSR. Private property was seized, and the Soviet government used brutal methods to punish opposition. These policies sparked a rebellion in Turkmenistan, and in 1927 the Soviets lost control of the republic to a national resistance movement called the Turkmen Freedom.

After reclaiming the Turkmen SSR in 1932, Stalin executed thousands of Turkmenistan's Communist leaders—including the president and the premier—whom he accused of helping the nationalists. After the terror of the 1930s, the Communist regime in Ashkhabad became completely obedient to the central Soviet government in Moscow.

Meanwhile, another international conflict was brewing in Europe. The western Soviet Union was devastated by World War II (1939–1945), when Germany invaded with a huge military force. Fierce fighting destroyed factories, farms, and cities throughout western Russia and Ukraine. After the war, the Soviets built new plants in central Asian cities, including Ashkhabad and Chardzhou. A work force made up of ethnic Russians and ethnic Ukrainians emigrated to the Turkmen SSR to take advantage of new jobs in the republic.

Most Turkmen, however, remained rural and nomadic. Despite the immigration of factory workers, the Turkmen SSR remained one of the Soviet Union's most isolated republics. Foreigners, and even Soviet citizens, were forbidden to visit most of the region, and the Soviet government also would not allow most Turkmen to travel outside the republic.

• The End of the Communist Era •

During the 1960s, Muhammetnazar Gapurov, the head of the Turkmen Communist party, emerged as one of the most conservative Communists in the USSR. Gapurov worked hard to stop

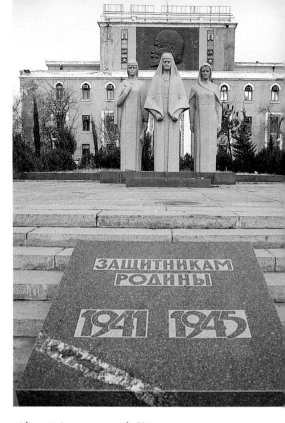

(Above) **A monument in Krasnovodsk honors Turkmen who died during World War II (1939–1945).** (Below) **Travelers buy U.S.-made soft drinks from a stand in Ashgabat's railway station. With reluctance, the Communist leaders of Turkmenistan accepted new economic policies in the 1980s that allowed more foreign goods into the country.**

a nationalist movement among the Turkmen. He also opposed any attempt to lift restrictions on Islam, which many nationalists favored as the basis of a future independent government.

In spite of the republic's isolation, economic development continued in the region. New irrigation projects diverted water from rivers to collective farms, many of which began growing fruits and vegetables instead of cotton. During the 1970s, the Soviet government also developed the region's energy resources, including oil and natural gas.

The Soviet leader Mikhail Gorbachev began several new policies after coming to power in 1985. *Glasnost* allowed more open criticism of the Communist party and of the country's economic system. *Perestroika* eased government control over many small businesses, which could now set their own wages, prices, and production schedules. Turkmen Communist leaders, however, were slow to adopt these reforms. Annamurad Khodzhamuradov, who became the Turkmen SSR's leader in 1986, remained loyal to the Soviet government but never accepted Gorbachev's reforms.

In the late 1980s, many Soviet republics attempted to gain their independence from Moscow. In 1990, the Turkmen SSR declared that it would take greater control over local politics and economic policy. The government established the office of president and named Saparmuryad Niyazov to the post.

Many Soviet officials believed that glasnost and perestroika were leading to the breakup of the USSR. In August 1991, several of Gorbachev's opponents within the Communist party staged a **coup d'état** to seize power. At first, the conservative leaders of the Turkmen SSR—who were against changes in the Communist system—supported this action. But after the coup failed, the republic's government backed Gorbachev's return to power.

Vendors sell vegetables in an open-air market in southern Turkmenistan. Once under strict government control, farmers can now set their own prices for some foods and consumer items.

• Independence •

For the next few weeks, the Turkmen government remained loyal to Moscow. The republic's Communist leaders approved Gorbachev's efforts to preserve the Soviet Union. But these efforts proved futile. As the Soviet Union broke apart, President Niyazov declared the independence of Turkmenistan. In October 1991, the Turkmen government held a public vote on self-rule, which was overwhelmingly approved by the population. October 27 became the republic's official Independence Day. In December, the leaders of several republics formed the Commonwealth of Independent States, which Turkmenistan also joined.

Despite the fall of the Communist regime, Turkmenistan still has a state-controlled economic system. The Turkmen Communist party has changed its name to the Turkmen Democratic party and has declared itself in favor of private property and a market economy. Nevertheless, many large factories, oil-drilling operations, and mines are still in the hands of the republic's government. Most collective farms remain intact, with farmers owning little private land for the growing of crops or the raising of livestock.

The system of centralized planning has left Turkmenistan with a stagnant economy. President Niyazov has proposed selling small firms to private

Born in Ashgabat in 1940, Saparmuryad Niyazov was educated in Leningrad (now St. Petersburg, Russia), where he graduated with an engineering degree. Niyazov's rise through the ranks of the Communist party began in the 1970s. By the late 1980s, he was head of the Turkmen Communist party and in 1990 became the first president of the Turkmen SSR. Later, after the Soviet Union broke up, Turkmen elected Niyazov to be president of independent Turkmenistan.

(Below) **Young Turkmen make extra money by selling bottled drinks.** (Right) **A building in Ashgabat flies the new Turkmen flag, which includes symbols of the Islamic religion and a decorative strip representing the country's famous hand-woven carpets.**

owners, but by 1993 this process had barely begun. To improve their prospects, many Turkmen favor an alliance with Iran, a strict Islamic state with which Turkmenistan has historic trading ties. Others seek cooperation with Turkey, a nation that is rapidly modernizing and that has close links with Europe and the Middle East. Turkmenistan may also steer a new, independent course away from the Commonwealth of Independent States and its neighbors in central Asia and the Middle East.

CHAPTER THREE

Making
a Living in
Turkmenistan

Before its independence, Turkmenistan was one of the poorest regions in the USSR. The republic relied on the Soviet central government to provide investment and a market for Turkmen goods and natural resources. Despite the breakup of the Soviet Union, the economies of Russia and Turkmenistan have remained closely tied. For example, Turkmenistan still ships most of its oil and natural gas through Russia.

Turkmenistan is now looking for foreign partners to help it modernize its industries. The most important of these new partners is Iran, which will be linked with Turkmenistan by a new railroad.

On a large farm near the capital, farmhands use machinery to gather and roll bales of hay.

Iran and Turkmenistan have made arrangements for the joint development of Turkmenistan's energy reserves. Iran is also planning to build a new, satellite-based communications system for its central Asian neighbor.

Turkmenistan has joined other central Asian republics—as well as Iran, Turkey, and Pakistan—in a regional economic council. This group aims to increase investment in the area and to improve trade between central Asia and the Middle East.

• *Agriculture* •

As the Russian Empire extended its control into central Asia, Turkmenistan became a hub of cotton cultivation and export. Raw cotton grown on farming estates along the Amu Darya supplied textile factories in distant Russian cities. During the 19th century, cotton remained the region's most important product.

(Above) **A bearded shepherd tends a flock of sheep on a steep mountain slope.** (Below) **Workers pile up huge mounds of raw cotton, which supplies textile mills in nearby former Soviet republics.**

Chardzhou

Gaurdak

Krasnovodsk

Nebit-Dag

ASHGABAT

Mary

Kara Kum Canal

TURKMENISTAN'S ECONOMIC ACTIVITIES

Industry		Thermal Energy	
Textiles		Natural Gas	
Building Materials		Herding	
Coal		Fruits and Vegetables	
Oil		Cotton	
Oil Refining			

Under Soviet rule, agriculture in Turkmenistan underwent drastic changes. Traditionally a nomadic people, the Turkmen were permanently settled by the government on state-owned collective farms during the 1930s. With new fertilizers, machinery, and irrigation systems, these collectives were able to produce larger yields of grain and cotton.

By the 1980s, many farms were switching to the raising of livestock and the growing of vegetables, grains, and fruits. These crops, and the privatization of farms, will improve the region's food supply. With the fall of Soviet authority, however, the governments of Turkmenistan and Uzbekistan are disputing rights to the water needed for large-scale farming.

For centuries, the nomadic Turkmen have also tended large animal herds. Collective farming has led to a more settled way of life for farmers and their livestock, which include cattle, sheep, goats, camels, and horses. Turkmenistan is also home to the Karakul sheep, whose soft, curly wool is fashionable throughout the world. Turkmenistan also exports horses, including the Argamak horse, a breed renowned for its beauty and endurance.

• Energy and Mining •

Throughout the 1970s and 1980s, while oil and natural gas production declined in the other energy-producing republics of the Soviet Union, output of these fuels rose rapidly in Turkmenistan. Turkmenistan is now third among the former Soviet republics in oil production, and the country extracts enough natural gas to export to foreign markets. Large oil fields lie along the Caspian Sea and near the town of Nebit-Dag, southeast of Krasnovodsk. Natural gas exists in this area, as well as near Mary. Pipelines run from these fields to Krasnovodsk, the major port for the shipment of both oil and gas.

A gas pipeline crosses the Kara Kum Canal near Ashgabat. Turkmenistan is building other pipelines to bring the country's oil and natural-gas resources to markets in the Middle East.

On a pedigree farm, a herder guides his special breed of horses to rich pasture and scarce watering holes.

The country still exports its oil to Russia for refining. But Turkmenistan has taken on new partners—including Iran—for foreign investment in this important sector. A new pipeline from Turkmenistan will carry natural gas across Iran to Turkey and to other nations of the Middle East.

Mines in Turkmenistan also produce small amounts of lignite coal, which powers electricity plants. The country's mineral resources include gypsum, mercury, sulfur, and the raw minerals used in making cement and glass. Extensive salt deposits exist near the Caspian Sea and in the Kara Kum Desert. Salt-processing plants operate at Chardzhou, Nebit-Dag, and Cheleken, a town on the Caspian Sea.

• Manufacturing and Trade •

In the past, most of Turkmenistan's people made their living from agriculture and from trade. Small industries—including carpetmaking and leatherworking—thrived in urban areas along central Asia's historic trade routes. In the 19th century, the Russian Empire built new silk factories in Turkmenistan, where raw silk has been produced for centuries. Under Soviet rule, several cities in the Turkmen SSR grew rapidly as new factories began to operate and as workers arrived from other parts of the USSR.

Turkmenistan has a long tradition of making fine hand-woven rugs. This Turkmen works at a plant in the capital.

GAMBLING WITH THE KARA-BOGAZ GOL

During the 1970s, scientists discovered valuable mineral deposits in western Turkmenistan beneath the salty waters of the Kara-Bogaz Gol (gulf). In 1980, Soviet officials decided to dam the channel that links the gulf with the Caspian Sea and allow the gulf to evaporate. This action would permit the mining of the bay's sandy floor. Planners also sought to reduce the amount of water being taken from the Caspian Sea for irrigation of central Asia's farmland.

By 1983, the Kara-Bogaz Gol was completely drained of seawater. After the water evaporated, large deposits of salt remained. Blowing winds carried the salt to farms and pastures in western Turkmenistan. The mixture of salt and soil increased water evaporation, making it necessary for Turkmen farmers to use even more water to irrigate their crops. The salt deposits in the soil also caused sterile patches to form where nothing would grow.

Instead of reducing the amount of irrigation water taken from the Caspian Sea, the gulf drainage project increased farmers' dependence on the sea. As a result, the mining project was abandoned in 1984, and the Kara-Bogaz Gol was allowed to refill. The salt damage to the region's fertile soil has remained, however, and local farms suffer from a continuing shortage of water. By draining the Kara-Bogaz Gol, Soviet officials caused a long-term agricultural and environmental problem that independent Turkmenistan is still struggling to resolve.

In the early 1980s, the Soviets built a wide dyke to close off the Kara-Bogaz Gol from the Caspian Sea.

Among thriving enterprises in Ashgabat are a large bakery (above), *where fresh, hot loaves of bread are stacked and sorted, and a clothing factory* (below), *where machines help workers to cut fabric.*

Manufacturing still makes up the smallest sector of Turkmenistan's economy, with factories providing only about 15 percent of the nation's production. For most heavy industry, the Turkmen government has decided to maintain the system of central planning and ownership. Although some firms will be sold to private owners, most large companies will remain state property.

Turkmenistan's biggest manufacturing business is the processing of natural resources, including oil and natural gas. With the discovery of oil near the Caspian Sea, the Soviet government built refineries in Krasnovodsk. After World War II, new plants in Krasnovodsk and Ashgabat also began producing cement and other building materials. Chemical factories—which refine a variety of raw minerals into useful construction materials and agricultural fertilizers—were built in central Turkmenistan and along the Caspian shore.

Plants in Ashgabat, the largest industrial center, process food, build heavy machinery, and make glass. Ashgabat factories also produce silk as well as hand-woven Bukhara carpets, which are exported around the world. Cotton grown in the Murgab and Amu Darya valleys supplies textile mills in Ashgabat, Chardzhou, Mary, and Gaurdak, a city on the Amu Darya.

Foreign trade will be an important ingredient in Turkmenistan's future, and the country needs outside investment to develop its export industries. A new railroad linking Turkmenistan and Iran will provide access to the markets of the Middle East. Nevertheless, Turkmenistan still conducts most of its trade with Russia and with its central Asian neighbors. Turkmenistan sells natural gas, oil, and cotton products to Russia. Imports include foodstuffs, heavy machinery, steel, construction materials, and vehicles.

CHAPTER FOUR

What's Next for Turkmenistan?

Although Turkmenistan has broken free of the Soviet Union, independence is bringing difficult challenges. With many Russian managers and workers emigrating, Turkmenistan will have to rely on a smaller and less skilled labor force. The country also needs foreign investment to develop and process its minerals and energy sources.

Many experts worry that new economic and social problems will bring the central Asian republics under the influence of radical Muslim governments in Asia. For example, across the southeastern border of Turkmenistan lies Afghanistan, where ethnic cousins of the Turkmen have brought an Islamic government to power after overthrowing a Communist regime.

A strong Islamic political party—the Islamic Renewal movement—emerged in central Asia in the fall of 1991. Organized in Turkmenistan and in each of the other Muslim republics, the group seeks a stronger role for Islam in the governments of the region. Although members of the former Turkmen Communist party still control the government,

A new department store in downtown Ashgabat offers shiny bicycles for sale.

Turkmenistan's new constitution allows opposition parties to participate in an advisory body known as the People's Supreme Council.

Under these social and political strains, Turkmenistan's people may draw closer to strict Islamic movements in Afghanistan and Iran. Another possibility is that the Turkmen will follow the example of Turkey, a nation that has preserved Islam while remaining close to European nations and pursuing a modern way of life.

A woman checks the bottling process at a dairy in Ashgabat.

FAST FACTS
ABOUT TURKMENISTAN

Total Population	3.9 million
Ethnic Mixture	72 percent Turkmen 10 percent Russian and Ukrainian 9 percent Uzbek 3 percent Kazakh
CAPITAL and Major Cities	ASHGABAT, Chardzhou, Mary, Krasnovodsk
Major Languages	Turkmen, Russian
Major Religion	Islam (Sunni branch)
Year of Inclusion in USSR	1924
	Fully independent state; member of Common- wealth of Independent States since 1991; member of United Nations since 1992

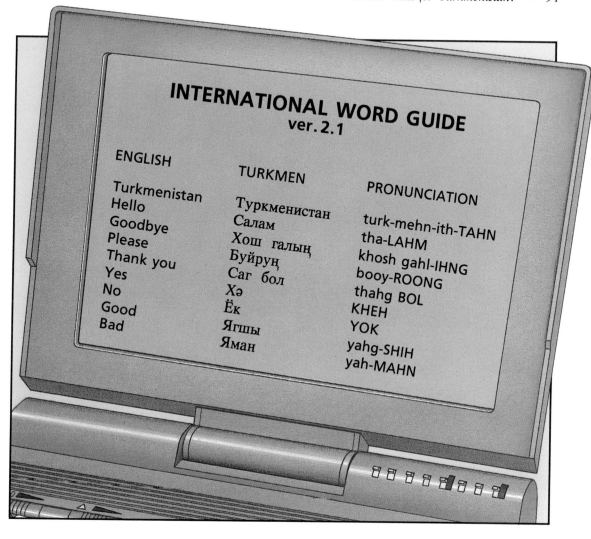

INTERNATIONAL WORD GUIDE
ver. 2.1

ENGLISH	TURKMEN	PRONUNCIATION
Turkmenistan	Туркменистан	turk-mehn-ith-TAHN
Hello	Салам	tha-LAHM
Goodbye	Хош галың	khosh gahl-IHNG
Please	Буйруң,	booy-ROONG
Thank you	Саг бол	thahg BOL
Yes	Хә	KHEH
No	Ёк	YOK
Good	Ягшы	yahg-SHIH
Bad	Яман	yah-MAHN

Turkmenistan's leaders must also decide how best to use the country's oil and mineral resources and how to modernize its industries and farms. The largest markets for Turkmenistan's cotton, oil, and natural gas are among neighboring nations that formerly belonged to Soviet Union. For this reason, Turkmenistan's main concern will be developing a prosperous common market with its Muslim neighbors in central Asia. As the country emerges from its historic isolation, however, it is finding the path to stability and prosperity to be a difficult one.

annex: to add a country or territory to the domain of another nation by force.

collective farm: a large agricultural estate worked by a group. The workers usually received a portion of the farm's harvest as wages. On a Soviet collective farm, the central government owned the land, buildings, and machinery.

Commonwealth of Independent States: a union of former Soviet republics founded in December 1991. The commonwealth has no formal constitution and functions as a loose economic and military association.

Communist: a person who supports Communism—an economic system in which the government owns all farmland and the means of producing goods in factories.

coup d'état: French words meaning ''blow to the state'' that refer to a swift, sudden overthrow of a government.

ethnic Russian: a person whose ethnic heritage is Slavic and who speaks Russian.

ethnic Turkmen: a person whose ethnic heritage is Turkic and who speaks Turkmen.

ethnic Ukrainian: a person whose ethnic heritage is Slavic and who speaks Ukrainian.

glasnost: meaning ''openness,'' the Russian name for a policy of easing restrictions on writing and speaking.

Wearing traditional clothing, a bride walks to her husband's house in a Turkmen village.

industrialize: to build and modernize factories for the purpose of manufacturing a wide variety of consumer goods and machinery.

khan: the leader of a central Asian domain, called a **khanate**, who ruled Turkic, Mongol, or Tatar peoples.

Oguz: an ethnic Turkic people who, in the 7th century A.D., began settling in Afghanistan, Iran, Turkey, and central Asia.

Well-wishers greet the arrival of the first Boeing jet acquired by Turkmenistan's new airlines.

perestroika: a policy of economic restructuring introduced in the late 1980s. Under perestroika, the Soviet state loosened its control of industry and agriculture and allowed small, private businesses to operate.

Russian Empire: a large kingdom that covered present-day Russia as well as areas to the west and south. It existed from roughly the mid-1500s to 1917.

Russian Turkestan: a region of central Asia inhabited by Turkic peoples that came under Russian control in the 18th and 19th centuries.

A greenhouse in the capital offers vocational students a chance to plant and harvest their own crops.

Silk Road: an ancient trade route that passed through central Asia, linking eastern Asia to the Middle East and Europe.

Tekke: an ancient clan of ethnic Turkmen that has become one of the largest and most powerful groups in modern Turkmenistan.

Transcaspia: an independent state established in southern central Asia in 1919. It survived only five years and was replaced by a Soviet republic.

Transcaspian Region: a military zone established by the Russian Empire in the area of modern Turkmenistan in the late 19th century.

Turkmen Soviet Socialist Republic: a republic founded in 1924 by the Soviet government and made a part of the Union of Soviet Socialist Republics. It was replaced in 1991 by the independent state of Turkmenistan.

Union of Soviet Socialist Republics (USSR): a large nation in eastern Europe and northern Asia that consisted of 15 member-republics. It existed from 1922 to 1991.

United Nations: an international organization formed after World War II whose primary purpose is to promote world peace through discussion and cooperation.

At a rug factory near Ashgabat, workers roll a finished piece back and forth to strengthen the weave.

• *Photo Acknowledgments* •

Photographs used courtesy of: pp. 1, 2, 5, 8 (left and right), 9, 10, 16 (bottom), 18, 19 (top), 20 (right), 21 (top), 22 (left), 24 (top and bottom right), 25, 40, 42 (top), 44 (bottom), 45, 47 (top and bottom), 48, 50, 53, 54, 55, © H. Huntly Hersch; pp. 6, 20 (left), 52, Naomi Duguid/Asia Access; pp. 12 (left and right), 16 (top), 17 (left), 19 (bottom), 21 (bottom), 23 (left), 24 (bottom left), 26, 28 (right), 29, 33, 34, 35, 36 (top and bottom), 37, 39 (left and right), © Yury Tatarinov; pp. 13, 23 (right), 38, 42 (bottom), 44 (top), 46, RIA-NOVOSTI/SOVFOTO; p. 22 (right), TASS/ SOVFOTO; p. 17 (right), © Shepard Sherbell/ SABA; p. 28 (left), Independent Picture Service. Maps and charts: pp. 14-15, 43, J. Michael Roy; pp. 30-31, 50, 51, Laura Westlund.

Covers: (Front) © Yury Tatarinov; (Back) © H. Huntly Hersch